D0536916

A FIRST LOOK AT AMERICA'S PRESIDENTS

THEODORE ROOSEVELT

The 26th President

by Josh Gregory

Consultant: Meena Bose
Director, Peter S. Kalikow Center for the Study of the American Presidency
Peter S. Kalikow Chair in Presidential Studies
Professor, Political Science
Hofstra University
Hempstead, New York

BEARPORT
PUBLISHING

New York, New York

Credits

Cover, © B Christopher/Alamy; 4, Courtesy of the Library of Congress; 5, Courtesy of the Library of Congress; 6, © AP Photo; 7L, © AA World Travel Library/Alamy; 7R, Courtesy of the Library of Congress; 8, Courtesy of the Library of Congress; 9T, © RRuntsch/Shutterstock; 9B, Courtesy of the Library of Congress; 10, Courtesy of the Library of Congress; 11, Courtesy of the Library of Congress; 12, © North Wind Picture Archives/Alamy; 13, Courtesy of the Library of Congress; 14–15, © Pierre Leclerc/Shutterstock; 16, Courtesy of the Library of Congress; 17T, Courtesy of the Library of Congress; 18, © spirit of america/Shutterstock; 19T, © RRuntsch/Shutterstock; 19B, © Matt Ragen/Shutterstock; 20T, © AP Photo; 20B, Courtesy of the Library of Congress; 21T, Courtesy of the Library of Congress; 21B, © North Wind Picture Archives/Alamy; 22, Courtesy of the Library of Congress; 23T, Courtesy of the Library of Congress; 23B, © Betty Shelton/Shutterstock.

Publisher: Kenn Goin
Editor: Jessica Rudolph
Creative Director: Spencer Brinker
Design: The Design Lab
Photo Researcher: Jennifer Zeiger

Special thanks to fifth-grader Lucy Barr and second-grader Brian Barr for their help in reviewing this book.

Library of Congress Cataloging-in-Publication Data

Gregory, Josh.
   Theodore Roosevelt: the 26th President / by Josh Gregory.
      pages cm.—(A first look at America's Presidents)
   Includes bibliographical references and index.
   ISBN 978-1-62724-557-9 (library binding)—ISBN 1-62724-557-X (library binding)
   1. Roosevelt, Theodore, 1858-1919—Juvenile literature. 2. Presidents—United States—Biography—Juvenile literature.
I. Title. II. Title: Theodore Roosevelt, the twenty-sixth President.
   E757.G75 2015
   973.91'1092—dc23 [B]   2014034604

For more information, write to Bearport Publishing Company, Inc., 45 West 21st Street, Suite 3B, New York, New York 10010. Printed in the United States of America.

10 9 8 7 6 5 4 3 2 1

CONTENTS

Taking Action

Theodore Roosevelt was always taking action. As a boy, he worked hard to make himself healthy. As president, he worked to make the country stronger. He also made it a better place for all Americans to live.

Theodore Roosevelt was known as a strong leader.

Theodore Roosevelt was the 26th president. He served from 1901 to 1909.

Getting Over an Illness

Theodore Roosevelt was born in 1858 in New York. As a child, he had very bad **asthma**. Sometimes he even had to go to the hospital. Theodore exercised a lot, however. He also spent lots of time outdoors. He became stronger. This helped him overcome his illness.

Theodore's family nicknamed him "Teedie."

Teedie spent much of his childhood in this house in New York City.

Teedie loved to go hiking. He drew pictures of the wildlife he saw.

As a child, Teedie went mountain climbing and tried many sports. By the time he was in his twenties, he was strong and healthy.

7

Starting Out

When Theodore Roosevelt grew up, he worked in **politics**. At age 23, he was **elected** to the New York state government. There, Roosevelt worked hard to make laws that helped people. Yet he also made time for outdoor adventure.

Roosevelt as a young man in the 1880s

Roosevelt took many trips to North Dakota. There, he hunted, rode horses, and raised cattle.

Roosevelt hunted buffalo and other animals in North Dakota.

Rough Riders

In 1898, the United States went to war against Spain. Roosevelt led soldiers in the war. He and his soldiers were called the Rough Riders. The Rough Riders won important battles.

Roosevelt

Roosevelt led the Rough Riders (above) into battle for control over Cuba. The Americans won the Spanish-American War.

The Rough Riders rode horses into battle in Cuba.

Roosevelt

American newspapers had stories about the Rough Riders. This made Roosevelt a famous war hero.

Becoming President

After the war, Roosevelt went back to politics. In 1900, William McKinley was elected president. Roosevelt was his vice president. Sadly, McKinley was shot and killed a few months later. This meant that Roosevelt would be president.

McKinley was shot while he was in Buffalo, New York.

Roosevelt was 42 years old when he became president. He was the youngest president in history.

13

Roosevelt in the World

Roosevelt played a big role in the world as well. In 1905, he helped end a war between Russia and Japan. A year earlier, he had workers begin digging the **Panama Canal.** This would be a shortcut for ships between the Atlantic and Pacific Oceans.

The war between Russia and Japan was called the Russo-Japanese War. Roosevelt helped end the war by talking to the leaders of both countries.

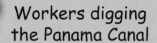
Workers digging the Panama Canal

Roosevelt made sure that the United States had a strong navy. He knew the navy would be even stronger when ships could use the Panama Canal.

North America

Atlantic Ocean

N
W   E
S

Panama Canal

Pacific Ocean

South America

The Panama Canal is located on a narrow strip of land that connects North and South America.

Remembering Roosevelt

Roosevelt kept helping people even after he left office. He continued to be a leader in politics. People listened to his ideas. Today, we still see his ideas in action.

Roosevelt

Roosevelt's face is carved into Mount Rushmore, in South Dakota. The other presidents shown in the sculpture are George Washington, Thomas Jefferson, and Abraham Lincoln.

This national park in North Dakota is named after Roosevelt.

Today, millions of people visit the parklands Roosevelt helped protect. About 14,000 ships cross the Panama Canal each year.

The Panama Canal today

TIMELINE

Here are some
major events from
Theodore Roosevelt's life.

1858
Theodore Roosevelt is
born in New York City.

◄──────┬──────────────┬──────────────┬──────────────┬──────
      1860   **1870**   **1880**   **1890**

1881
Roosevelt is elected
to the New York
State Assembly.

1901
Roosevelt becomes president after William McKinley is killed.

1900
Roosevelt is elected vice president.

1904
Work begins on the Panama Canal.

| 1900 | 1910 | 1920 |

1898
Roosevelt forms the Rough Riders and fights in the Spanish-American War.

1919
Roosevelt dies at his home in New York.

"We must dare to be great."

"The only man who makes no mistakes is the man who never does anything."

When Roosevelt was young, his family called him Teedie. When he got older, his nickname changed to Teddy.

Roosevelt was a distant cousin of Franklin D. Roosevelt, who became the 32nd president.

Teddy bears were named after Teddy Roosevelt.

1858 ❀ THEODORE ❀ 1919
❀ ROOSEVELT ❀

22

GLOSSARY

asthma (AZ-muh) a medical condition that makes it difficult for a person to breathe

elected (i-LEK-tid) chosen by vote for an office in government

Panama Canal (PAN-uh-mah kuh-NAL) a path dug across the country of Panama that lets ships travel between the Atlantic and Pacific Oceans

politics (POL-uh-tiks) the actions involved in governing a city, state, or nation

wildlife (WILDE-life) wild animals living in their natural setting

Index

Read More

Rappaport, Doreen. *To Dare Mighty Things: The Life of Theodore Roosevelt.* New York: Disney-Hyperion (2013).

Rosenstock, Barb. *The Camping Trip That Changed America: Theodore Roosevelt, John Muir, and Our National Parks.* New York: Dial Books for Young Readers (2012).

Learn More Online

To learn more about Theodore Roosevelt, visit **www.bearportpublishing.com/AmericasPresidents**

About the Author: Josh Gregory writes and edits books for kids. He lives in Chicago, Illinois.